THE LAST LEHMAN BROTHERS ANALYST CLASS

THE UNTOLD STORY OF LEHMAN'S
2008 ANALYST CLASS - BANKING'S
LOST GENERATION

DAN GUS

© 2024 Dan Gus. All rights reserved.

First Edition

This is a work of narrative nonfiction based on interviews conducted between 2021-2024. While the events described are real, names, physical descriptions, and certain identifying details have been changed to protect the privacy of individuals. Some dialogues and scenes have been reconstructed from participants' recollections.

The interviews were conducted remotely and transcribed to the best ability. While every effort has been made to ensure accuracy, quotes may contain minor variations from the exact words spoken due to the nature of memory, translation, and transcription. Some quotations have been edited for clarity while maintaining their essential meaning.

No part of this book may be reproduced, distributed, or transmitted in any form or by any means, including photocopying, recording, or other electronic or mechanical methods, without the prior written permission of the author, except for brief quotations in critical reviews and certain other noncommercial uses permitted by copyright law. For permission requests, please contact the author.

The views and opinions expressed in this book are those of the author and the individuals interviewed. They do not necessarily reflect the official policy or position of any financial institution, employer, or organization mentioned within.

Every effort has been made to verify the accuracy of the information contained herein. However, neither the publisher nor the author assumes any responsibility for errors, omissions, or contrary interpretations of the subject matter.

CONTENTS

	Intro	1
1	The Fall of a Giant: The Largest Corporate Bankruptcy in U.S. History	5
2	Finding My Lost Class: A 13-Year Search	9
3	Who Made the Cut: The Class of 2008	13
4	Never Ignore a Good Warning Sign	19
5	Where were you when?	27
6	Being lucky	35
7	The Non-Bankers	41
8	What's 8% of 8? Overcoming Imposter Syndrome	49
9	The High Cost of Ambition	55
10	Risk & Reward: Changed Perspectives	63
11	Breaking the Glass Ceiling: Gender in the Trading World	69
12	Beyond the Finish Line: Career, Family, and the Personal Cost	75
13	Picking Up the Pieces	83
14	Afterword	93
	Acknowledgments	97

Intro

Canary Wharf, London

August 2008

Waiters in white gloves balanced trays of hors d'oeuvres as they moved across the plush carpet stretching to the huge windows of the 26th floor of the Lehman Brothers tower.

At twenty-eight, fresh out of college and after a string of minimum-wage jobs, I finally felt I'd made it. I had been accepted into one of the largest investment banks in the world — the premier league of bankers.

Thursday, September 11th, 2008

The conference room on the ground floor of the Lehman

building. Rumors about an approaching bankruptcy or rescue of Lehman by the American government. The second-in-command at the London branch, known for his aggressive style, stands before us, 100 students of the analyst class, explaining that we are strong, that Lehman is strong, and despite attempts to strike us down, we would get through this together*.

Friday, September 12th, 2008

Graduation day for the 2008 analyst class. At 5:00 PM, an email was sent saying that the notifications regarding the units we were chosen for had been delayed by a few days and we will receive an update later.

Monday, September 15th, 2008

After a weekend of tense anticipation, I woke up early that Monday morning. A single email in my inbox announced what would become the largest bankruptcy in history - the collapse of what, until moments before, had been my workplace

Within a few hours

Farewell emails circulated, with the understanding that the company's servers would soon be locked. A class of 100 analysts, from dozens of countries, with an acceptance ratio of 1 to 1,000, said goodby, each forced to reconsider career paths we'd thought were set.

2024

Life rarely asks if we want to change course. This is the story of 100 people who stood at the threshold of what seemed guaranteed success in a ruthless industry, only to have that certainty shattered overnight. Their stories raise questions that resonate far beyond banking:

Why did they choose this path?

Did they chase the same dream again, or find new ones?

What does success mean when your chosen path disappears?

And most importantly:

What happens when we are forced to rewrite our futures?

This is the story of some of the 100 people whose fates changed on the morning of September 15, 2008.

* Months later, we learned a bitter truth: while our London leaders promised survival, the American branch was already withdrawing funds, ensuring better bankruptcy terms for themselves at London's expense.

CHAPTER 1

The Fall of a Giant: The Largest Corporate Bankruptcy in U.S. History

Once a titan of Wall Street, Lehman Brothers embodied the American financial dream. From its humble beginnings as a dry goods store in 1844, it had grown into one of America's most respected investment banks. By the mid-2000s, it ranked fourth among U.S. investment banks, behind only Goldman Sachs, Morgan Stanley, and Merrill Lynch.

In early 2007, Lehman's stock hit an all-time high of $86

per share, valuing the firm at nearly $60 billion. With 26,000 employees across the globe and major hubs in New York, London, and Asia, Lehman dominated fixed-income trading and played kingmaker in major mergers and acquisitions. Few suspected this financial giant would soon become the face of the 2008 financial crisis.

The Last day — Waiting for a Bailout

As Lehman teetered on the brink of collapse, Wall Street held its breath, expecting another government rescue. After all, the federal government had stepped in to save Bear Stearns just months earlier. But this time, the script would play out differently.

In a twist worthy of Shakespeare, Bank of America, which had been negotiating to buy Lehman, suddenly changed course. Instead of rescuing Lehman, they announced plans to acquire Merrill Lynch, another struggling Wall Street titan.

Meanwhile, American insurance giant AIG was also in trouble. In a decision that would spark fierce debate and reshape financial history, regulators deemed AIG "too big to fail" while letting Lehman collapse. Some viewed it as necessary triage to prevent economic collapse; others saw it as blatant favoritism.

Our class watched as the institution's collapse became

inevitable. The financial certainties they once relied on crumbled alongside Lehman's stock price. It was a harsh lesson in the unpredictability of markets and the seemingly arbitrary outcomes of a crisis.

To understand what happened next, we need to break down the crisis itself.

Understanding the Collapse: A Simple Guide to Complex Failure

Picture the housing bubble as Wall Street's wildest party ever -

The Guest List: Banks handed out mortgages like party invitations – no RSVP required, everyone was welcome.

The VIP Section: Lehman Brothers wasn't just attending- they were running the show, turning risky mortgages into "exclusive" financial products.

The Price of Entry: These mortgages were bundled and sold as premium investments, but they were built on shaky ground.

Last Call: When homeowners started defaulting, the music stopped. Those "exclusive" financial products? Suddenly worthless.

Lights On: The housing market crashed, and Lehman's big bets went bust.

The Aftermath: Lehman's gamble on the perpetual

housing boom led to the largest corporate bankruptcy in U.S. history — a reminder that even the biggest players can fall when they take reckless risks.

The London perspective

While New York dominated the headlines, Lehman's European headquarters in London became ground zero for international operations. A cultural and operational chasm opened between the offices as the crisis deepened. As New York focused on damage control in the U.S. market, the London office felt increasingly isolated and abandoned.

On September 15, 2008, the unthinkable happened: Lehman Brothers filed for bankruptcy. Overnight, thousands of employees, including hundreds of fresh-faced analysts in London who had barely started their careers – found themselves out of work.

This is where our story truly begins — not with the big-picture economics or the high-level negotiations, but with those young analysts whose promising careers collided with the largest corporate collapse in American history. We were more than statistics in a historical event, we were people whose lives were about to change forever.

CHAPTER 2

Finding My Lost Class: A 13-Year Search

The Lehman collapse couldn't have come at a worse time. My wife and I had just moved to London, our shipping container of belongings had arrived that weekend, and we'd just signed a two-year lease. The timing was devastating. The situation was particularly precarious because neither of us had a European passport. The clock started ticking: 60 days to secure a new job in London before my work permit expired. The odds were daunting — I would be competing with 15,000 newly unemployed finance professionals, most with European citizenship. My choices were stark: throw myself into that competitive fray or pack up and head back home.

Fast forward 13 years

In 2021, a question began nagging at me: what had become of the analyst class of 2008 — my class? Where had the winds of fate scattered us?

For those less familiar with investment banking, the "analyst class" refers to a group of recent graduates hired by a bank to start their careers as junior financial analysts. These entry-level positions are highly competitive and typically filled by top graduates from elite universities.

Investment banks hire analysts in "classes" or cohorts, usually bringing in a new group each year. These analysts typically commit to a two-year program, during which they work long hours, learn the intricacies of financial modeling, and support senior bankers in various tasks such as creating presentations, conducting research, and assisting with deals.

Think of it as a pressure cooker designed to transform bright graduates into banking professionals. While known for its punishing hours and steep learning curve, it was seen as a guaranteed path to high-paying careers in finance, consulting, or business leadership.

Our class of 2008 had the misfortune of perfect timing — we

walked into this pressure cooker just as the global financial system was imploding. None of us could have predicted how that timing would shape our careers and lives.

The Hunt Begins

How do you track down people after thirteen years? People who've potentially changed names, countries, and careers?

I started simple: creating a folder on my Google Drive called "+13" - marking the years since 2008. That turned out to be the easy part.

What followed was a three-year odyssey: mapping out over 100 analysts scattered across the globe, reaching out one by one, and conducting hour-long interviews over Zoom and Teams. While I had prepared a standard set of 15 questions, each conversation took on its own direction.

The real challenge proved to be finding these people. I dug through my Gmail archive and found an old Excel sheet listing about 50 analysts. I turned to LinkedIn, sending out simple messages: "Hey, remember me from the Lehman analyst class?" While some responded eagerly, many messages vanished into the digital void.

After the first article about the project went live, I tried again with the holdouts. Some finally bit.

The Lucky Break

Around my twentieth interview, fate smiled. One interviewee had kept the holy grail — our analyst class CV book. Back then, Lehman compiled all new analyst resumes into this book for recruiting managers. Through a stroke of luck, my contact had obtained it from a Nomura (the Japanese bank that bought parts of Lehman's London operations) HR manager who unearthed it during a 2018 clear-out. Thanks to him, Finally, I had the complete roster of the Class of 2008.

A Note on Privacy

Bankers are known for being private, especially about their personal lives and choices. This reality shaped my approach to telling their stories. Some made their privacy concerns clear upfront, others during our chats. To honor their trust, I've changed all names and identifying details. The # on parentheses marks the order of the interviews.

Their stories are real; their identities are protected. What follows is a chronicle of lives disrupted and rebuilt, of dreams shattered and reshaped, and of lessons learned in the crucible of crisis.

CHAPTER 3

Who Made the Cut: The Class of 2008

Understanding who we were is crucial to understanding what we became. After conducting dozens of hours of interviews, I gained an intimate glimpse into the diverse tapestry of personalities and backgrounds that made up our class. The stories that emerged were as varied as they were fascinating, and while it's impossible to capture every nuance, I'll highlight the key characteristics that defined the 2008 analyst class through several distinct personas

The Selection Process

Investment banking recruitment was a gauntlet designed to identify a specific type of excellence. The process centered heavily on interviews and case studies, with candidates facing what felt like an endless series of trials. A typical candidate underwent five to ten interviews at the bank's local branch, culminating in what we called the "four by four" — a grueling process where four candidates were interviewed over four hours by four senior executives.

The odds were daunting: Usually, only one candidate from each group was selected. Industry data suggested an acceptance rate of roughly one in five applicants, with thousands initially submitting their resumes. But the process had a fundamental flaw: there was a natural bias toward selecting candidates who mirrored the interviewers' profiles rather than those best suited for the role.

The Demographics: A Global Talent Pool

While most analysts hadn't listed their nationalities on their resumes, the London class had been predominantly Western European, with British candidates forming the largest group. About 30% came from Asian countries, India being the biggest contributor. Our newly established Russian branch brought in several analysts from former

Soviet states. A small number of Americans joined us, though most preferred starting at Lehman's U.S. offices.

In terms of gender, the class was 30% women and 70% men – relatively balanced for an industry historically dominated by men.

Educational Pedigree: The Best and Brightest

While the demographic makeup of our class was diverse, the educational backgrounds showed remarkable consistency. Each analyst held at minimum a bachelor's degree from elite institutions like Oxford, Cambridge, LSE, INSEAD, Yale, and Harvard. But these weren't just academic machines — they excelled in everything from competitive sports to advanced mathematics. Indian analysts, in particular, often came with eye-popping credentials, highlighting their rankings from their country's most competitive universities.

The Great Divide: Numbers vs. People

The analysts were prepared for different roles within the bank. Early in the analyst training program, I was struck by the realization that many of them had studied advanced economics or mathematics and had substantial financial backgrounds. Academically, the group could be broadly divided into two categories: the "numbers people" destined for trading roles that relied on complex mathematical models, and the "social sciences people", typically placed on client-facing desks that required strong interpersonal and relationship-building skills.

Career Motivations

Some analysts had been following the markets since their teenage years and had always known banking was their calling. Others discovered the field through friends or recruitment events, drawn more by prestige and high salaries than genuine interest. These "discovered bankers" often competed for roles they understood only superficially.

Economic Backgrounds: A Tale of Two Classes

Perhaps the most striking divide was invisible on our resumes. A substantial number had come from affluent backgrounds — evident in their prestigious boarding schools, elite universities, and upper-class hobbies like horse riding. In contrast, the "first-generation professionals" analysts were often first-generation university graduates from low-medium income families.

When the financial crisis hit, this background gap became a chasm. Those without family wealth to cushion the blow faced particularly difficult choices. Their future wasn't just about career trajectory — it was about financial survival.

This diversity of backgrounds would prove crucial in the aftermath of the collapse. How each analyst responded to the crisis often reflected not just their professional preparation, but the life experiences and safety nets they brought with them. As we would soon learn, sometimes the most valuable skills in a crisis aren't the ones taught in banking programs.

CHAPTER 4

Never Ignore a Good Warning Sign

My own warning came from an unlikely prophet. Prior to joining Lehman, I had worked under an economist specializing in macroeconomic analysis. He introduced me to the fundamentals of capital markets. In February 2008, I was accepted into the Lehman Brothers analyst program, and I was offered a transfer to the London branch due to cutbacks in the Israeli office. When I called my former boss to share my news about relocating, his laughter should have been my first clue. He'd never been one for tact. "Good luck", he said, "but you'll be back here by January 2009." Drunk on dreams of an international career, I dismissed his warning.

His prediction proved eerily precise. On October 31st, just 60 days before his predicted date, I was on a plane back home.

My story wasn't unique. As I interviewed my former classmates, I noticed a recurring pattern of ignored warnings and dismissed doubts. Here are some of their stories:

Early warning signs

Oliver (#33), a German analyst who joined in 2008, had worked in real estate securitization where the bank sometimes offered 99% financing — meaning developers only needed to put down $1 for every $100 of property value. "Looking back, it seems insane", he recalled. "But that was business as usual back then." He overheard discussions about splitting the bank's troubled assets into a "bad bank" — a potential strategy to prevent the collapse. Oliver mentions that when he questioned the project's financing structure, which seemed illogical to him, almost immediately, he was removed from the project team. On the day the bank collapsed, he realized there was no chance of saving his position.

Willow (#36) noted that the warning signs began even during the hiring process. "Usually, employees would receive a contract in April or May, but Lehman delayed. Eventually, I received the contract in June, signed it, and moved to London two days before the course began in 2008. I should have known something was wrong — this was much less organized than my internship."

Kunal (#32), interviewed from Mumbai, where he manages a hedge fund, recalled the moment he realized something was up. He lived near the company's offices in Canary Wharf. Starting in September, during his walks around the area, he repeatedly saw senior executives from the bank sitting in pubs with likely recruiters from other banks. "And I thought to myself, senior directors will be the first to find jobs, and our turn in the chain is very far off." In his case, that prediction proved true, and around the time I was on the plane back to Israel, he was on a plane back to India.

Seraphina (#34), the daughter of immigrants, did her internship at Goldman Sachs but wasn't a good fit. "I didn't like them, and they didn't like me." At Lehman, she met different people, and after the 2008 analyst course, she was supposed to take a year off before being placed as a trader. She was assigned to perhaps the most unusual trading desk possible: Uranium trading. According to her, there was a time when Lehman maintained uranium reserves in Canada for trading. She too saw clear warning signs. "And my friends were telling me: you need to get out. Immediately. But I kept telling them: all the senior managers are telling me everything will be fine."

The Cobbler's Children Go Barefoot

As industry leaders, investment bankers and financial advisors should have been able to spot an impending crisis. Many of them failed to do so when it came to their own workplace.

Bruno (#35) from the UK recalled, "The funny thing was that the entire team on the trading floor was very bearish (expecting a decline) about the market, and in the month before the collapse, all the traders were watching their trades become super profitable. We just didn't expect the firm itself to crash."

Amara (#26) describes a similar situation. She remembers in the weeks before the collapse, traders on the trading floor made the most basic mistake in investing — becoming emotionally attached to an idea and buying more and more Lehman shares, believing the bank would survive. Emma (#2) observed the exact same thing. "I remember the stock price collapsing, and people kept buying more and more shares because they believed the situation would improve."

Seraphina (#34) clearly remembers the moment when the company's stock dropped below the $2 mark, a psychological barrier that signaled recovery was no longer possible. At that moment, Seraphina was on the trading floor — a vast space with hundreds of people seated at long rows of desks. "Suddenly, everyone fell silent, as if in one synchronized, single moment."

Too Big to Fail

As the bank spiraled downward, we all clung desperately to the "Too Big to Fail" — the belief that the U.S. government wouldn't let an institution managing such vast assets collapse, and would step in with whatever financial support was needed to prevent it. In Lehman's case, the government decided not to intervene, and the idea of "Too Big to Fail" collapsed, plunging the world into a new economic crisis.

Isaac (#41) sensed that something bad was going to happen and consulted a friend. The friend told him, "You work in a bank. Banks don't go bankrupt."

Willow and her friend visited their designated desk where they were supposed to be stationed the weekend before the bankruptcy and asked the senior manager if they would still have their jobs on Monday. He replied, "On Monday, we will be something. Maybe not Lehman, maybe Bank of America, maybe Barclays, but definitely something." As it turned out, she was laid off.

The Suspension of Trading with the Bank

A bank's survival depends entirely on maintaining active trading relationships and credit lines with other institutions. When a bank loses its credibility, other banks stop trading with it to protect themselves.

Felix (#19) was one of those who always dreamed of working in banking. He grew up in a Nordic country, began his university studies there, and enrolled for a year of study in London, where he realized that the city offered the most exposure to financial markets. He left his degree program in his home country and started anew in the UK. On the night of Sunday, September 14th, he was at dinner with a friend who traded at a major international bank. The friend told him that all credit lines to Lehman had been cut a few days earlier, and trading with Lehman had effectively ceased.

Drake (#40) remembers that a few days before September 15, he visited some Lehman Brothers traders he knew from his internship a year beforehand. The traders told him, "No one is willing to trade with us (Lehman) anymore."

David (#15) received a call on Saturday, September 13, from a friend who worked at another bank and was called in to unwind positions (cancel deals) with Lehman. That was the moment he realized everything was falling apart.

Perhaps the person who can best describe the refusal to

face reality is Nisha (#29). She still holds a position in the banking industry. In her self-introduction, I immediately noticed how worn out she seemed. "I've been in the same role for 15 years, selling very specific products. Boring." Her choice of the word "boring" spoke volumes. By July 2008, mere weeks before our training program was set to begin, her father asked her if she was sure about her choice. "Lehman's situation doesn't look good." Her response captured all our youthful hubris: "What, are you kidding? I just got the best job I could imagine."

Apparently the hardest warnings to hear are the ones that threaten our dreams.

CHAPTER 5

Where were you when?

Life-changing moments become permanently etched in our memories.

Psychologists call it a "flashbulb memory" — a vivid recollection of where we were during momentous events. This is a special type of memory where people remember details about traumatic or dramatic events with remarkable clarity — like where they were and what they were doing when the event occurred. There are several unique occurrences that spark the phenomenon.

Emotional impact
When we experience a sudden, traumatic event, our brain releases chemicals like adrenaline, literally burning the moment into our memory.

Historical and cultural significance
When personal crisis intersects with historical events, the memory gets reinforced not just by individual experience but by collective remembrance.

Personal relevance and perception
People tend to remember events better when they are considered significant to them or the society they live in.

Repetition and conversation
An event that was widely covered in the media and became a public conversation topic for a long time strengthens memory through frequent repetition and discussion.

Surprise and uniqueness
Surprising and unusual events tend to be remembered better than everyday occurrences because they break what we expect to happen.

These psychological principles played out vividly in our experiences. Many people in finance clearly remember the day Lehman Brothers collapsed. For the analyst class, this event contained all the necessary ingredients to be indelibly etched in their minds.

My own flashbulb memory plays like a film I've watched too many times. That final weekend remains crystal clear. All of us were in limbo, waiting to learn our fate. We were all waiting to hear what would happen. It was clear to me that my continued stay in London depended on my job at the bank. Just days earlier, my life had seemed perfectly arranged. That Sunday, I wandered along the Thames with my wife, both of us trying to pretend it was just another beautiful London afternoon.

Monday morning arrived with brutal clarity. At 6:00 AM, I went to our living room to check emails. I can still see my desk overlooking an English yard in West Hampstead, and the email that announced the company had declared bankruptcy. There would be no miracle rescue, no last-minute salvation. I went to wake up my wife and start replanning our future.

For each analyst, the memory crystallized at different moments. Some recalled the events leading up to the collapse more clearly than the collapse itself.

Jenny (#23), who has since become a senior banker in Asia, can still picture the day her internship ended in 2007 — a full year before the collapse. Each accepted intern received a large white envelope with their contract details, including the most important part — the annual salary and signing bonus. The new hires were so happy that they went out together to celebrate at a club in London, holding their envelopes and celebrating a future that then seemed guaranteed.

Kai (#12) recalled a contrast between two events — a formal cocktail party on the 26th floor where all the senior managers came to pick their preferred candidate, followed a week later by cleaning a local cemetery for a community service event. He remembers thinking that one moment you're touching the sky, and the next, everything is dark. While cleaning the cemetery, he realized that if this was the event to close the course, the bank's situation was likely very poor.

Today, it sounds almost surreal, but in a time when mobile browsing was just becoming available, members of the analyst class received the news over several hours rather than immediately.

In what might be the most darkly comic memory, Zara (#30) managed to completely miss the collapse. On Monday morning, the day the bankruptcy was announced, she took the train towards work. When she arrived at the station near the office, she received a free newspaper, folded it with the main page hidden and continued on her way. When she arrived at the Lehman building, PWC accountants, who were chosen to lead the bankruptcy process, were handing out leaflets to employees asking everyone to stay in their places. Zara, who didn't understand the note's significance, assumed it was just another audit. When she reached her desk, she met a friend from the analyst class who looked particularly pale. She asked him, half-jokingly, half-seriously, "What happened? Did someone die?" Only then did she realize the magnitude of the event. She unfolded the newspaper and saw the headline, likely making her the last employee to learn about the bankruptcy.

Raj (#44) remembers the apartment he shared with several other analysts who came to the class from India. They sat in the living room all night, and he remembers the image of the bankers coming out of the fateful meeting where it was announced that Bank of America would purchase Merrill Lynch — sealing Lehman's fate for bankruptcy.

Kai (#12), from one of the Nordic countries, woke up after a long weekend of partying. He decided that in the absence of certainty, it was better to enjoy the moment. While still in bed, he received a text message from his older sister asking if he was okay. He didn't understand what she meant, but a few minutes later, he learned about the bankruptcy. It had already been made clear to him that the department that was about to hire him no longer intended to recruit more employees, so he understood that his chances of surviving at Lehman or whatever would be left of it were very slim.

Wyn (#28) spent the weekend before the collapse in Paris, waiting for what he considered the "golden news" – the possibility that Lehman would be acquired by Bank of America. When he realized on Sunday that Bank of America had started purchasing Merrill Lynch, he knew that Lehman was headed for bankruptcy. On Monday morning, he woke up to a flood of messages on his BlackBerry. When he reached the kitchen, his mother told him, "Lehman collapsed. It's just terrible."

I asked each interviewee about their first conversation after hearing the news. The answers revealed how young we all were — most called family.

Theo (#20) called his father, who had previously worked in finance but switched to teaching. His father simply told him, "These things happen. Good luck."

Marco (#46) was still sleeping in his rented apartment. His father woke him up with a phone call at 7:00 AM. Marco told his father he planned to sleep in because he didn't need to be at work until the afternoon. "You should read the news and call someone because I'm not sure you're going to work today".

Flashbulb memories are not always entirely accurate, but they are strongly imprinted in the mind due to the combination of intense emotions, historical significance, and repetition in the media and conversations.

Sometimes the most interesting memories are the ones our minds choose to bury.

I caught up with Nisha (#29) on a Friday during trading hours - typically a calmer time for markets. But this interview had a few brief interruptions for urgent trading calls, shedding light on how dynamic and demanding life on the trading floor is. Nisha apologized several times, and in between, we managed to sneak in a few sentences. In the interview, she didn't clearly remember what happened on the day of the collapse. Her flashbulb memory wasn't sharply imprinted.

Months after our conversation I shared the article published about the project to everyone I had interviewed up to that point. The next day, I received two WhatsApp messages from Nisha:

[15.9.2023, 09:55]: I met u at the station outside my work, and we both burst into tears on the road with people watching! Very vividly remember

[15.9.2023, 09:55]: From my mum! Clearly, I had totally repressed this memory. Apparently, I did arrive home to my parents' crying :)

Memories hide not because they're forgotten, but because they're too precious - or too painful - to casually recall.

CHAPTER 6

Being lucky

When a life-changing opportunity appears at just the right moment, is it truly luck?

The day Lehman offered me the position after my London interviews, I felt on top of the world. Six months later, that euphoria had turned to despair. As I spoke with my former classmates, one question kept surfacing: How much had luck shaped our divergent paths after Lehman? More Specifically, I asked each of them: Do you believe that fate, karma, or luck shaped the events that followed the collapse?

Asking a group of mathematicians and scientists about

karma might seem counterintuitive. These were people trained to explain everything through cause and effect. Yet their answers revealed surprising insights about fate and fortune.

It took nearly two years to finally connect with Amara (#26). Our dance began in November 2021, came tantalizingly close to happening in 2022, only to slip away again. Finally, in September 2023, the meeting materialized. When we did meet, I understood why it had taken so long. Her energy was off the charts, she seemed to pack a month's worth of achievement into every day. Now running an innovative tourism venture, she offered a precise insight when I asked about luck: "I believe in hard work. Hard work puts you in a position where good luck can find you."

Nia's story (#4) proved Amara's point. Like me, Nia was on a work visa with a countdown to expiration the moment we lost our jobs. In her darkest moment, she reached out to her father, who offered support and even volunteered to fly in from their home country to help her pack up. But he added one crucial question: "What are you going to do about it?"

This became Nia's life mantra — rejection is redirection. She could either abandon her dream or fight for it. Four days after the collapse, on a Saturday night, Nia snuck back into the office for a simple reason: she needed to print her resume and didn't have a printer at home. What happened next reads like a movie script. She ran into the head of Lehman's equity division.

"Hey! Are you an analyst?" he asked.

A startled Nia replied, "Yes."

"Come with me, we need help processing data."

Instead of heading home, Nia spent the entire night and following days at the office, crunching numbers, ordering pizzas, making coffee runs – doing whatever was needed to make herself useful. This chance encounter secured her a spot among the roughly ten "survivors" from the class of 100 analysts who stayed with Lehman.

Coming from a mixed religious background — Christian father, Buddhist mother — Nia considers herself religious but primarily believes everything happens for a reason. She credits both the universe and her father for leading her back to the building that fateful September 22nd night.

For Kai (#12), his entire future pivoted on a mere ten-pound note — the price difference between two flight tickets that placed him precisely where he needed to be. The weekend before the bank's collapse, already anxious about the future, he calculated his odds:

- Either Lehman would go bankrupt and he'd lose his job, Or

- Another bank would acquire Lehman, implement immediate layoffs, and he'd still lose his job.

Feeling suffocated, he decided to escape London for the weekend. He had two options: visit a friend in Prague or one in Dublin. Checking flights, he found Dublin was ten pounds cheaper than Prague. Anticipating unemployment, he chose the cheaper option.

After enjoying a pleasant weekend with his friend in Dublin, Kai returned to London on Sunday, September 14th. The next day, overwhelmed by loneliness and the need to find solutions, he started reaching out to everyone he knew. His Dublin friend responded, saying that their weekend companions — the local Google team — thought Kai would be a good fit and encouraged him to apply.

Kai started at Google's Irish headquarters on December 10th. Ten days later, Google announced a hiring freeze due to the economic crisis. "Talent matters", Kai reflects, "but in 2008, luck trumped talent."

Amid this tale of financial ruin, there's one unexpected story of romance. Oliver (#33) remains grateful for his termination because it led him to his wife. After losing his job, he secured a new position starting in November 2008. With just a few thousand euros in savings, he retreated to his parents' home in Asia.

Restless and alone, he took to the hiking trails. Tourism

was slow then, with few travelers around. After dinner in a small town, he noticed a backpacker smiling at him during his evening walk. Seeking an opening, he invited her to dinner - despite having already eaten earlier that evening.

When he shared his Lehman story, she – an Australian backpacker – found it fascinating, though it was completely new to her. They continued traveling together for several weeks. Months after he returned to Europe, she altered her travel plans to join him. They married and now have two children.

"My wife wants us to go backpacking again", he said, "but I tell her I've got a good job now — we'll have to wait for the next economic collapse." Perhaps they'll get lucky again.

What seems like misfortune in the moment can reveal itself as a blessing in disguise.

Consider Arjun (#14): a brilliant engineer from India who'd graduated from one of the country's most prestigious universities. He began his career at a major hardware company but discovered his true interest lay in trading. His exceptional abilities earned him a place at Lehman, and his talent helped him survive the collapse, securing a position at Nomura when they acquired part of the operations.

"We faced layoffs every quarter", he recalled. "I made it through December but was cut in March 2009." His visa expired, forcing him back to India, though his skills and determination eventually brought him back to a prestigious bank in London.

But here's where luck shows its peculiar sense of humor. Arjun felt he'd missed out — until he read a newspaper article in 2011. It revealed that his former group had attempted some questionable financial engineering involving tax refunds from a European country – refunds nearly equal to that country's entire annual tax revenue. The scandal erupted, with one of his former managers facing criminal charges and testifying before the Senate. Arjun realized his "setback" had actually been a fortunate escape. "You can't force things to happen", he reflected.

Time and again, my former colleagues, whether they'd ultimately thrived or struggled, spoke of how their paths had been shaped by circumstances beyond their control. The most valuable lesson from this extraordinary story is recognizing that no matter how smart or talented you are, complete control is an illusion.

As Ricky (#11), one of the rare few who remained with the bank observed, "I didn't find my path; my path found me."

CHAPTER 7

The Non-Bankers

In the aftermath of the collapse, I deliberately chose to work only with tangible, physical products. The Lehman debacle had left me thoroughly disillusioned with the banking system and financial markets. I wanted nothing further to do with finance.

When I began this project, I carried what turned out to be a false assumption — that most of the analysts would have distanced themselves from the industry like I did, especially after experiencing such trauma. The interviews revealed a surprising truth: Only about 20% actually left banking.

You Can Check Out Anytime You Want, but You Can Never Leave

The industry retains its professionals through its iron grip, with high compensation making it difficult to leave. The desire to leave often conflicts with a simple reality: dependence on both the high salary and the standard of living it provides.

Speaking from her hometown in Western Europe, Sophia (#10) shared how her life had taken unexpected turns. A Covid-era breakup had left her navigating the complexities of dating during lockdown. A graduate of Economics and Business Administration from one of London's top universities, Sophia had her pick of banks but chose Lehman because "the culture seemed more welcoming."

She had just returned to London the weekend before the collapse, preparing for the work week ahead when the bankruptcy announcement hit. "Going to the office that Monday morning was surreal. The elevator ride to my new department on the upper floors felt like the longest of my life, I had absolutely no idea what to expect." To her relief, she learned her division would remain intact and her position was secure, though she weathered the market instability like everyone else.

After two years, feeling overwhelmed by the workload, Sophia decided to move back to her hometown to be closer to family. It was then that she considered a career change. Before choosing economics, she'd been drawn to history and art, but her parents had steered her toward a more "practical" degree. She found what seemed like her dream job — managing an international bank's art collection.

Reality hit hard. "When I saw the salary offer, I was stunned. It was barely enough to cover my monthly rent payment, let alone other expenses." Ultimately, she chose to stay in banking.

Elena (#24) spoke with me on a hectic Monday morning, fresh from the daily battle of daycare drop-off. "With a three-year-old and a ten-month-old, mornings are always unpredictable", she said. It took about fifteen minutes for her initial reserve to melt away as she opened up about her journey.

After several years in banking, she took time off to volunteer at an orphanage in South America — a decision that worried her parents, who watched their daughter's carefully planned future seemingly unravel. Upon returning, she pivoted to entrepreneurship, launching a successful food stall with her former roommate — the same one who'd been with her the day Lehman collapsed.

The venture gained significant media attention, and they planned to expand into a restaurant. However, after calculating the investment needed and potential ownership dilution, they decided to close rather than lose control of their creation.

Banking's gravitational pull proved strong, Elena returned to banking, landing a position at a major international bank where she still works today. When I ask why she came back, she answers without hesitation: "The salary", then adds, "I was also tired of working with people who lacked motivation."

She paid a price for her detour — accepting a lower management position due to her time away from the industry. "I'm still trying to convince the bank that business experience outside banking is valuable experience."

The analyst program left little to chance. On day one, after a carefully orchestrated 30-minute networking session, we were led to two classrooms on the lobby floor. Name plates awaited us at assigned seats. I was placed next to Philip (#5). We were likely the oldest in the class, both approaching our late 20s. The opening exercise required introducing the person beside you, making Philip one of my first connections. It quickly became clear why we were seated together — beyond our age and receding hairlines, we were both military veterans from different countries.

After a decade in finance, Philip bought a large SUV and embarked on a cross-continental adventure with his wife and three children (then 14, 11, and 8). They traveled through Vietnam, Thailand, Nepal, Cuba, Guatemala, Uruguay, Peru, Costa Rica, and Chile. Yet even this grand escape proved temporary, he too eventually returned to finance.

The Switchers

Ben (#1) was our class superstar. An Ivy League graduate, he arrived with deep financial knowledge and plenty of confidence. While I struggled to grasp basic concepts, he was engaging lecturers in debates about advanced mathematical solutions. Eventually, Ben left London to pursue a medical career in his home country. Though uncommon, he wasn't alone. A few classmates also chose to start fresh in new fields after their first degree.

After six years of medical school, he began specializing in radiology at a European hospital. During his residency, former university friends offered him a position at their AI-focused statistical analysis company. Looking back, he considers himself fortunate: "I didn't waste a decade in finance before finding my true calling." The crisis accelerated his transition to medicine and life sciences, where he feels he belongs.

Emma (#2) carried the weight of our conversation even over a phone call. The anonymity allowed for more candid conversation. She described experiencing what I'd call depression in the months following the collapse — the dreary London winter made worse by the isolation of being unemployed while everyone around her worked. When I asked how she filled those long solitary days, she laughed, "Mostly shopping."

After a six-month job search, she landed a position in institutional sales at a major corporation. "It's the kind of job you stick with", she reflects. "The base salary isn't spectacular, but the benefits are solid." She adds: "I may not have the most impressive career, but I'm content." When I challenge this self-assessment, pointing out her senior position at a major company, she explains, "I just feel like I haven't made a real difference in the world." She compares herself to friends in consulting and crisis management — jobs she perceives as having greater impact.

Liam (#27) rode the tech wave, co-founding a health food startup in India. Despite raising a million dollars in funding, the company couldn't achieve sustainable growth. After closing the business, he found his niche joining one of India's rapidly expanding tech companies as Chief of Staff. When the company needed product managers, he transitioned into product management. Five years later, he moved to a similar role in Singapore, where he's now settled.

And the Winner Is...

Grace (#8) begins our conversation with infectious energy, eagerly offering a virtual tour of her island home, complete with the requisite sprawling lawn and oceanfront pool. "I live in paradise", she jokes, "and ironically, I'm not even a beach person."

Her path to paradise started with boredom. Looking for a hobby, she took flying lessons. After getting her pilot's license, she started thinking about ways to fly without the expense. When an airline friend mentioned their pilot shortage and company-sponsored commercial training program, she jumped at the opportunity.

Now she maintains her love of flying by piloting cargo routes two to three times weekly, island-hopping with five or six stops to deliver goods - mostly fish. "I'll never look at sushi the same way", she laughs, having spent countless hours loading and transporting fish to island restaurants. But for Grace, flying remains her escape, bringing joy to each workday.

CHAPTER 8

What's 8% of 8? Overcoming Imposter Syndrome

The television series "Industry" which premiered in 2020, offered a dramatized glimpse into the world of young bankers. This British-American creation by Mickey Down and Konrad Kay follows a group of young graduates as they enter the competitive world of finance in London, facing professional, personal, and ethical challenges at the prestigious investment bank "Pierpoint & Co." The show explores the complex world of banking and investment, where every decision can lead to either major success or crushing failure. These young professionals have to navigate office politics, the relentless demands of clients, and their intense drive to prove themselves.

While my banking colleagues dismissed it as sensationalized drama, I found myself captivated by something they'd missed — its honest portrayal of imposter syndrome.

If you're already familiar with the term, feel free to skip ahead to the next paragraph. For those who aren't, imagine feeling like a fraud despite clear evidence of your success. It's a psychological condition where accomplished people believe they don't deserve their achievements and live in fear of being "exposed". Think of it as your inner critic on steroids — no matter your accomplishments, you attribute success to luck or others' misunderstandings.

"Industry" features characters who exhibit classic signs of imposter syndrome. One the leading character, Harper Stern, faces immense pressure at work and struggles to prove herself in a cutthroat environment. Even though she's talented and successful, she often feels like she doesn't belong or deserve her success, fearing her weaknesses will be exposed.

When it comes to imposter syndrome, there are two types of people: those who admit to it and those who don't. But, honestly, I think a big part of surviving in the working world involves managing imposter syndrome.

Standing in front of the mirror before my London

interviews, I barely recognized myself. At 28, wearing my first proper suit and a tie I'd learned to knot just days before, I was about to "demonstrate" my extensive knowledge of finance, knowledge that felt anything but extensive.

Of the four interviews, one began promisingly. The interviewer posed a classic brain teaser: "Calculate the daily hamburger sales in Florida." I used all the techniques I'd practiced beforehand: round numbers, logical assumptions, and arrived at a decent answer. The interviewer was pleased, even pointing out that I hadn't considered hamburger sales at tourist spots like amusement parks.

Then came the question: "What's 8% of 8?".

I froze. I was so used to using round numbers that I said, "Well, 10% is 0.8, so 8% must be a bit less." But the interviewer wanted an exact answer. At that moment, the world seemed divided into two types: those who could instantly calculate such figures, and those who would forever struggle. I didn't know, and imposter syndrome hit me hard. How could I possibly get the job if I didn't know the answer?

The interviewer made a note - a physical reminder of my failure. The rest of the interview continued, but my mind kept working on that problem. Eventually, I figured it out. As we were wrapping up, I thanked him for the interview and said, "By the way, the answer to that earlier question is 0.64." Saved—for the moment.

Even the most impressive credentials couldn't ward off imposter syndrome. Samuel (#37), now at a prestigious hedge fund, embodied the quintessential "disheveled professor" — sporting a thick beard and untamed hair, radiating an infectious enthusiasm.

Yet even he battled self-doubt: "I found myself at a meeting with a finance minister from the Emirates, a senior representative from the UK, and several top executives. My first thought was: I don't belong here. But then I quickly reminded myself: being here means you belong." He's been "belonging" for 15 years now.

When Aron (#22) joined the research department, he found himself surrounded by PhDs — a credential he notably lacked. The insecurity was immediate. "But I'm naturally more optimistic than most people. I tend toward optimism", he explained. "Stay with anything long enough, and mastery becomes inevitable." It was at that point Aron realized that even his manager didn't have a PhD.

Aron decided to use the COVID-19 lockdown period to pursue his own PhD. While the world slowed down, this kid from India, who had always dreamed of living in London, ensured he would never feel inferior again. Today, he's Dr. Aron.

Elena (#24) took a different perspective. When I asked her what advice she would give herself in hindsight, she said, "I'd give the same advice to myself as I would to every woman: believe in yourself. There were so many times I found myself in rooms full of men in suits, wondering, how will anyone take me seriously?" She found a way to manage and is still thriving in the field today.

We often meet people who seem to exude confidence, and instantly we feel inferior to them, forgetting that maybe only a few decisions and twists of fate separate us.

Perhaps the most enlightening story came from Noah (#9). At one of his jobs, he worked with a former Lehman Brothers employee. This individual's name had come up in the legal cases involving the bank's extravagant spending during its final days, and so, his employment letter had been public knowledge for a while. The senior manager joined Lehman about a year before the collapse. His base salary was around £200,000, not unusual, but his guaranteed annual bonus for the first year and the year after was £5.8 million. Noah attended several meetings with this executive and couldn't reconcile the compensation with the person. He described the man as a typical New York banker, full of bravado but with nothing apparent to justify such a huge paycheck. "At that moment, I realized—no matter how senior or esteemed someone might be, at the end of the day, everyone cooks with water."

That might be the realization that can help all of us who struggle with imposter syndrome. In banking, as in life, sometimes the most confident people in the room have the least reason to be. And those who question themselves the most have the least reason to doubt.

CHAPTER 9

The High Cost of Ambition

American investment banks have long been known for their ruthless organizational culture. In the world of investment banking, promotion opportunities come at a premium, and client service means one thing above all else: being available around the clock, ready to respond at a moment's notice. The salaries are high, and correspondingly, the "price of admission" that employees, especially juniors, pay is particularly steep.

The true cost of this culture became tragically clear in 2013. Morad "Mo" Hafiz, an intern at Bank of America Merrill Lynch in London, collapsed and died from an epileptic seizure after working nearly 72 hours without rest. His death wasn't just a personal tragedy — it was an indictment of an entire system. The incident shocked the banking community and media, leading to widespread discussions about the harsh working conditions often endured by interns and analysts. Only then did banks start implementing policies to limit working hours and ensure adequate rest periods

Learning the Hierarchy

Like interns in many fields, analysts were expected to learn on the job. Unlike some industries, however, the treatment they received ranged from merely poor to absolutely brutal. Beneath the bank's polished exterior lay a culture of fierce competition and ruthless advancement.

"There were a lot of elbows and a very cutthroat vibe", Sophia (#10) recalled, noting that while she could endure some of the competitiveness, extreme behaviors were harder to tolerate. "I remember when a junior analyst accidentally touched a trader's chair on the trading floor, and the trader went ballistic."

David's (#15) experience illustrated how even the most capable analysts found themselves reduced to performing mundane tasks. After landing a job at Nomura months after the collapse, he spent his days changing the colors of presentations from Lehman's subdued green to Nomura's bright red - Probably the most expensive paint job you can find.

Hugo (#18) mentions that in the days leading up to the bankruptcy, the U.S. branch transferred large sums of money, possibly including pension funds from the London branch, to its own control. He still remembers a particularly brutal conference call between the American and British teams, during which the Brits asked: "How could you abandon us like this? Why won't you share some of the funds back?"

Everyone at Lehman knew "Lehman's spirit" and "the Lehman way of doing business." The American representative said coldly — "The only thing we'll share with you is our deepest sympathy."

Raj (#44) discovered that even the welcome gift had teeth. Unfortunately for Raj, his bonus was structured as a loan that had to be repaid if he did not fulfill the contract. Although the sum was "only" a few thousand pounds, Lehman's liquidators, who were trying to recover parts of the $600 billion in debt, didn't relent. They demanded that he repay the loan.

"I felt like I was being hunted down. They even found my new address in India, and I kept receiving demand and threat letters for a very long time." Raj recalled the immense pain: "With all the losses I suffered, I also had to pay what was, at the time, an enormous sum for me."

Senior Management

Though the open-plan office suggested equality — with most employees arranged in long rows — the bank maintained a rigid hierarchy with crystal-clear boundaries. A junior analyst knew that if they dared to respond disrespectfully to someone one or two levels above them, they would be seriously jeopardizing their future at the bank. Senior managers were typically distant figures, very busy, short-tempered, with whom one was expected to have minimal contact, and of course, to be fully available at all hours.

When the collapse came, these once-mighty managers lost everything — not just their jobs but their wealth, much of which was tied up in bank shares. Some of them understood the gravity of the situation and the responsibility they held towards their employees, while others, of course, crumbled.

The weekend before the collapse, Hugo's (#18) future boss informed him that the department he was supposed to work in would likely be acquired, and that his position was secure. Hugo spent the weekend without checking the news, only to find on Monday that the situation was very different. From that moment on, that manager avoided him, crossing to the other hallway whenever he saw him.

Jenny (#23), now a senior executive herself, remembers a Managing Director (MD), three to four levels above a starting analyst, who was always very tough and impatient with everyone. When Jenny went to the restroom on the morning of the collapse, she found that same MD on the floor, crying uncontrollably. She remembers approaching her, saying, "I'm so sorry for you", and even giving her a comforting pat on the back — something she would never have dared to do otherwise.

Mark's (#3) most vivid memory comes from a post-collapse visit. Mark approached a former senior executive and tried to strike up a conversation. The executive was sitting at a desk, deeply engrossed in a Minesweeper game. The senior didn't either respond nor acknowledged the conversation, and Mark simply retreated. Just days before, he was practically a demigod, and a week later, he was playing on the computer.

Samuel (#37) recalled the surreal atmosphere as managers stopped answering calls until one trader approached him and asked:

"What are you doing here"

"What do you mean, what am I doing here? No one told me not to come."

The trader, with uncharacteristic restraint for a trader, explained that most managers had lost their jobs and all their savings, so they had a few other things to deal with before worrying about the interns.

Our analyst class finished their training on Thursday, September 12th. Being in a pool of analysts without specific desk assignments meant we felt like orphans on the day of the collapse. No one really communicated with us or explained what would happen next.

As Oscar (#17) put it, "The only contact I had after the collapse was two months later, when I got a phone call telling me I'd been laid off, but would receive my salary through October."

The Disillusionment

The collapse shattered more than just careers — it demolished the very ideals that had drawn many to banking in the first place.

Aisha (#39) noted that the greatest impact on her was in terms of her loyalty to her workplace. "Before Lehman's collapse, I was sure I would be the most dedicated employee for years. On the day of the collapse, I realized that I need to maximize my situation at every given moment." Loyalty, she learned, is a one-way street.

Wynn (#28) vividly remembers the Thursday meeting

before the collapse: "A man stood before me and explained that Lehman's cash reserves would definitely last for two more years, and two days later, we were bankrupt. I thought to myself, I don't want to work in an industry that lies to you."

Hugh (#45), a mathematician by training, didn't grow up intending to be a banker. During a summer internship, he was exposed to the bank's operations and found the people around him to be smart and decent. "There were some very smart people doing things I thought were really cool". Hugh described the deep mistrust that was instilled in him after that "everything will be okay" speech. "If you have no idea what's going to happen at your job in two days, you're better off not being there. I'm now very, very skeptical of speeches by senior executives at staff meetings. Always".

CHAPTER 10

Risk & Reward: Changed Perspectives

For me each morning in London began the same way: a 7:00 AM dash through London's rush hour, followed by a 40-minute train journey to the heart of the financial district. During these commutes, I'd often reflect on Warren Buffett's wry observation that "Wall Street is the only place where people ride in Rolls-Royces to get advice from those who take the subway". Buffett's observation resonated deeply with my own experience at Lehman.

Replace "Wall Street" with "Canary Wharf" and "subway" with "Underground", and you have our story perfectly captured.

This paradox led to the central question driving my research: How had the Lehman collapse reshaped our class's relationship with risk over the subsequent fifteen years? Did they bounce back, or did it fundamentally alter their relationship with risk?

For me, the answer was clear. The collapse left me with a profound aversion to risk – any risk. Most notably, I stopped investing in the stock market altogether. After watching those glossy presentations and precisely calculated financial products evaporate into nothing, I kept my personal capital as far from risk as possible for years to come.

Today, Warren Buffett's words echo in my mind: "If past history was all there was to the game, the richest people would be librarians." My risk aversion, while emotionally comforting, was potentially costly. The mathematics of my caution proved sobering: modest $100 investment in the S&P 500 during the depths of September 2008 would have blossomed into $488 by September 2023, $345 after adjusting for inflation. A reminder of missed opportunities.

During my interviews, I broached the subject of risk appetite with each participant, particularly regarding their investment choices. It's not a typical question for bankers, former or current, but their responses were enlightening.

I found solace in discovering I wasn't alone in my newfound cautiousness. The crisis left lasting imprints on many of my colleagues' financial behaviors.

Kai (#12), who ultimately returned to his Nordic roots, cited academic research demonstrating how graduating into a recession can permanently depress lifetime earnings. But beyond the obvious financial setbacks, I believe these experiences fundamentally shaped how our generation approached economic decisions throughout their lives.

Zara's (#30) narrative crystallized this transformation. At 22, her path had seemed perfectly plotted - prestigious London banking position, promising fresh start. Then everything crumbled.

"The timing was awful", she told me. "My boyfriend broke up with me just as Lehman was collapsing. I couldn't tell which loss I was grieving more." She retreated to her native Moscow, fortunate enough to find someone to take over her London lease. "I left everything behind - the kitchenware, the bedding I'd just bought. I never thought I'd see London again."

Eight years later, something pulled her back to London. Over her new bank's multiple restructurings, she held on tenaciously, knowing she needed five years for permanent residency. She made it, coincidentally just as Russia's isolation from the West intensified. Now a British citizen, she still maintains a small apartment in Moscow her parents bought her – her safety net. "I would never sell that apartment. Lehman taught me humility", she reflected. "Without that experience, I'd probably be insufferably arrogant today."

David (#15), despite his current senior position in the investment industry, exemplified this acquired risk aversion. After Lehman's collapse, he went into pure survival mode. His first move was securing readmission to a British business school where he'd previously been accepted. He had no idea how he'd pay for it, but he bought himself a month's extension on the tuition deadline – just to keep his options open in London.

David continued showing up at Lehman's offices daily, emailing anyone who might assist, even before the next academic year began. Weeks later, on his way to a quantitative methods class, he got a call from Nomura. They needed someone who spoke German – he fit the bill. He walked away from his class that day and straight into banking again.

The early months were surreal - the environment was charged with fear. Friday layoffs became routine, with the dreaded 11:00 AM phone calls summoning people to the ninth floor. David still remembered being tense whenever his phone rang around that time.

The experience left deep scars. Despite marriage and a child, the whole family lived in a modest studio for a decade. He's never invested in stocks and describes himself as deeply risk-averse. "That feeling of scarcity, of needing money from my parents, it never really leaves you", he admitted.

Not everyone retreated from risk entirely. Nikhil (#42), speaking from his Asian office, still actively invests – partly because his role requires it. "Skin in the game", he explained, noting that a significant portion of his monthly salary goes into company funds, as is common practice in India's investment sector.

Many others found middle ground, often choosing index funds over individual stocks. As one former analyst put it, "The last thing I want is to bring my work home with me."

The "Teams" interviews revealed the fascinating locations of my former colleagues. When I asked Seraphina (#34) where she was, her answer – "A village in the French Alps" – caught me off guard. A third-generation British citizen from an Indian immigrant family, she and her husband (another Lehman alum) made the move during COVID, raising their infant far from London's financial district.

"We're definitely risk-averse," she admitted. "Our investment portfolio is probably too conservative. I'll be working until I'm 85 to live comfortably." But at least the Alpine views make up for it.

Dev (#43), who left finance, summed it up: "The biggest change after Lehman? I stopped planning more than a year ahead. I used to map out two or three career moves in advance. Now I know better. One year at a time is plenty."

It's not just about financial calculations, but about how we view the future itself. Sometimes the biggest risk isn't taking chances, but believing we can predict what comes next.

CHAPTER 11

Breaking the Glass Ceiling: Gender in the Trading World

This chapter presented a challenge. Despite my years of involvement in gender equality initiatives, I grappled with whether I could do justice to those experiences. I questioned whether I had the right perspective to tackle such a sensitive topic.

Ultimately, I decided to include this chapter out of respect for the women who shared their experiences with such remarkable candor.

The demographics told their own story: women constituted merely 30% of our analyst class, creating an inherent limitation in capturing their experiences. Towards the end of each interview, if the rapport allowed, I broached the subject of their experiences as women in finance.

As with all stories in this book, all names have been changed to protect privacy.

Nisha (#29) cut through any pretense with startling directness. When I delicately raised the topic of potential harassment, her response was unequivocal — "Women being treated poorly? Around me? With me? Absolutely. Any woman who's been in this industry for 15 years and claims she hasn't experienced it is flat-out lying."

Let's break this down from several angles, and we'll wrap up with Clara's story — a tale that touches on all these issues but still manages to offer a glimmer of hope.

The Old Boys' Club: Assumptions and Biases

Zara (#30) drew a sharp distinction between then and now: "My current firm is incredibly demanding, and discussions can turn fierce, but unlike the bank, it's purely about business performance. I don't feel like I'm treated differently because I'm a woman."

That said, Zara's acutely aware of the gender pay gap. She estimates a man in her position would be earning about 30% more. With her current career track, she hasn't entered a relationship yet and knows that when she decides to have children, she'll pay the "mommy tax" - the career impact of taking maternity leave.

Jenny (#23) says her current bank has been great about her maternity leaves, but she delicately mentions that at a previous job, "I had a boss who... well, let's just say he made some seriously inappropriate comments."

Networking in No Man's Land

The disparity became stark for Zara (#30) upon reaching senior levels. "The revelation struck when I discovered my former male intern colleague had secured a VP position two years ahead of me." Why? "It's a cakewalk for guys to network."

She points to pre-meeting small talk as a prime example. "The moment they start talking about last night's game, I'm instantly sidelined. I've noticed it's way easier to connect socially when there are more women around."

Seraphina (#34) landed in the notoriously tough world of investment banking. "I was the only woman in the department. Every weekend, the guys would visit strip clubs. On Monday, I'd get an earful about their escapades.

It was, without question, the toughest year of my life." She transferred to another bank as soon as she could.

From Microaggressions to Outright Sexism

Jenice (#48) weathered a constant stream of gender-based assumptions, particularly regarding her presence on the trading floor. "Once, I was sitting outside the global sales manager's office. A senior client manager who knew me from emails walked up and told me the lobby door was broken and I should call maintenance. He just assumed that as a woman near a big shot's office, I must be his secretary."

When I asked Elena (#24) about harassment, she said it never came from clients, "but from senior managers? Oh yeah." Her typical response? "I'd usually say it was getting late and I needed to head out."

You can't blame her for playing it safe when her job was on the line. "I should mention, some of my male colleagues at my level tried to step in and stop this behavior. They were promptly told the next day that if they kept interfering, they'd be out of a job."

When I pressed about other forms of mistreatment, she gave a disheartening response: "There was rudeness, disrespect, condescension, you know, the usual stuff every woman deals with in any workplace."

Jenny (#23) faced inappropriate sexual comments from

a manager at her post-Nomura job. Breaking from the industry trend of staying quiet, she reported him, and he backed off. Jenny believes her action not only helped her but protected future female employees. When I asked if she always managed to say no, she replied, "I can't recall a time I couldn't say no... well, maybe a few dicey situations at Christmas parties". Reading between the lines, it's clear there were times she felt pressured.

A Ray of Hope

Clara's (#7) story serves as both a culmination and a counterpoint to these experiences. Among all the graduates, she seemed most naturally suited for the trading floor's intensity. Ironically, everyone around her — parents and business school friends told her she didn't have what it takes to be a trader.

With the odds stacked against her, she decided to forge her own path. As someone who left home at 16, she was no stranger to doing things her way. I first met her when she was intently watching Lehman Brothers' plummeting stock, 3 weeks before the collapse.

Clara's big break came when her boss went on maternity leave, giving her a chance to trade serious volume much earlier than usual. This was her moment, and she seized it. But one of her toughest career moments also revolved around maternity leave — her own.

A significant portion of a trader's pay comes from annual bonuses tied to performance. After returning from maternity leave, Clara was invited to meet with an executive from the U.S. branch about gender equality. Just before the meeting, her manager dropped a bombshell: since she was out for 3 months, she'd only get three quarters of her bonus — not because she missed targets, but simply because she was on maternity leave. Furious, she went into the meeting with the executive, who asked for thoughts on equality. Clara, never one to mince words, told him point-blank that talk about gender equality is meaningless when you're docking her pay just for having a baby.

Clara ended up getting her full bonus that year.

These stories paint a complex picture. Each woman I interviewed faced barriers, biases, and exclusion in her own way — some fought back, some stayed quiet, some just tried to persevere. But they all shared one thing: they found a way to keep going.

Thanks to these trailblazers breaking into the boys' club, things will slowly but surely improve for women in finance.

CHAPTER 12

Beyond the Finish Line: Career, Family, and the Personal Cost

The recruitment ritual unfolds like a well-rehearsed theater production at elite universities worldwide. As graduation approaches, banks stage elaborate evening presentations featuring sharply dressed bankers, usually men, in suits and ties, showcasing their glamorous careers. They paint pictures of international prestige and astronomical salaries.

Yet somehow, no one ever says, "Just so you know, if you ever have kids, you might find yourself choosing between career growth and watching them grow." Or even the simpler truth: "We offer everything here — except a personal life."

Early in my tenure, my relatively new manager, barely a year into his role, initiated a defining conversation. He outlined the bank's binary task classification: urgent and pressing. The distinction, he explained with practiced irony, was that urgent tasks required immediate attention, while pressing ones needed completion before they were even assigned, or in other words — every email or request should be answered without delay.

My first real test came when developing a dynamic yield curve model. If you're unfamiliar with it, it's fine, just imagine a complex financial model requiring intricate calculations.

The assignment arrived with deceptive simplicity: "I need this model." The implications, however, would consume my entire weekend. It took two days to complete, with 17-hour workdays and multiple frustrating calls to an unhelpful London trader.

The parallels with military service were striking: your time belonged unconditionally to the institution. Theater tickets, family gatherings, and trips abroad: all of it becomes irrelevant when a task comes in, it is always either urgent or pressing.

My "compensation" for leaving banking ultimately rested on two pillars: precious final months with my father and irreplaceable years with my children.

A year after my return home, my father was diagnosed with terminal cancer and passed away within 10 months. If I'd stayed in banking, I imagine I would have kept working, and I would have barely seen him in his final months, not to mention that I wouldn't have been able to care for him as I did at the end.

The second comfort is ongoing. I got to watch my kids grow up. To be clear, I'm not here to romanticize the endless demands of parenting — it's a second full-time job, with tough conditions and zero pay. But it's a meaningful experience, both for the parent and especially for the child. And I know for certain I wouldn't have been there for my children in the same way if I'd stayed in banking.

My experience reflected a broader industry pattern.

When I speak to Noa (#8), he sounds relaxed in his Zurich office, just a 10-minute walk from the lake where he likes to swim in the summer. When I ask him about his path to banking, he laughs. "Some of our training cohort said they dreamed of becoming analysts at 15. How on earth do you know at 15 that you want to work in banking? I certainly didn't." In fact, he never thought he'd end up in banking. He decided to move back to Switzerland about seven years ago after his eldest son was born. The decision was triggered from an unexpected source. When his son was six months old, people started asking which school he was registered for in London, or, more accurately, which waiting list he was on. That's when he realized something didn't feel right about staying in London.

Ray (#21) struggles to articulate his feelings about his time at Lehman. When I ask what advice he'd give his younger self, he pauses. "Now that I have kids and a family, I realize I was way too consumed by work. I worked from seven to seven, but juniors were expected to socialize after hours, so I went out almost every night. Looking back, I'd have put more energy into what's actually important."

Several alumni were nearing 40 and either live alone or are in relationships but don't have kids. For some, the intensity of the work — the long, demanding hours — played a part. Aisha (#39) says, almost apologetically, "We decided not to have children. It's just a personal choice." She didn't elaborate, and I didn't press her.

Jay (#38) had what many would consider a successful career — surviving the financial crash and maintaining a position in London for a decade. But at 40, something shifted. He quit his London job and returned to his home country in Europe. His father had passed away a few weeks before our interview, and he was now caring for his mother, who was fighting cancer.

Through these interviews, I aimed to uncover what my classmates felt they had gained or lost in the wake of Lehman's collapse. Wynn (#28) has no doubt: he gained his father.

His story spans continents. Originally from Africa but raised and educated in Europe, Wynn had only visited his family's African business during vacations. "I was never groomed to take over the family business. I always assumed my career would head in other directions."

Just two days after the collapse, the desk manager he was set to join moved to a competing bank and offered Wynn a job. Wynn hesitated between this and another opportunity. "I had two great offers with good salaries, but I'd lost faith in finance."

His father suggested a different path: come to Africa for a week's vacation, take a breather, and decide from there. While still undecided, Wynn got yet another offer, this time from a venture capital firm. But he opted to join his father's business

Over the next decade, he worked alongside his father in Africa, learned the language, and fell in love with the country. After his father passed away five years ago, he took over as chairman of the family company. Wynn married three years ago and now has two children. His family mainly lives in Geneva, while he splits his time between Geneva and Africa. Besides running the family business, Wynn also serves on the investment committee of a Geneva-based fund.

Looking back, he says, "I still use my time at Lehman as an icebreaker in conversations. I didn't lose anything and gained an entire decade with my father." How can you put a value on a decade with your father?

Nisha (#29), not yet 40 when we spoke, said, "I'm already feeling burned out and imagine I'll move to a less demanding job in the future."

Mia (#6), the only one to mention leaving her career to raise children, decided to switch to a less time-intensive role after her second son was born and now works in regulation and audit at a local bank. She admitted honestly, "Yes, my job is interesting, and I'm constantly learning", but she wouldn't have chosen this field without the pressures at home. "This isn't the career I'll be in forever, but it's okay for now."

Hugh (#45) offers a perspective on the trade-offs: "For the biggest and most complex deals, you have to be in London. Where I am now is different — there are deals, but they're not as complex. It's a different level of commitment, and the pay is lower. Since my kids were born, I've started to re-evaluate my priorities. A demanding London job simply doesn't support a lifestyle with kids."

After COVID and recent years, it's harder to justify demanding physical presence from morning till night. "With us, you can work from anywhere, anytime. Attending your kid's school events is totally fine." Hugh seems genuinely happy with this approach.

Enzo (#31), towards the end of our conversation, mentioned his family is about to move, which would mean a one-hour commute each way and likely mean seeing his kids mostly on weekends. "There'll come a point where I'll have to make up for this," he hinted, suggesting that a lifestyle change might be in order. With the high salaries London offers, and hearing from so many finance professionals through this project, I can only hope he figures it out just before his kids grow up.

Elena (#24) loved her work but felt burnt out after five years. She tried transferring to another department and then immediately left. I asked if it was the long hours. "We worked from around 7:00 AM to 6:00 PM but we also had to entertain clients several nights a week. I'd get home at 4:00 AM after a night of drinking, and the cycle would repeat." She ended up going back to her original department.

Emma (#2) left banking years ago, and for her, Lehman is a distant memory. She still regrets one big compromise. "I remember skipping my best friend's wedding to study for an exam. Since then, I've learned to prioritize what really matters."

CHAPTER 13

Picking Up the Pieces

How does one rebuild when a global economic crisis has swept away not just a job, but an entire imagined future?

This was the first question that the final class of analysts at Lehman Brothers had to confront.

How do you make sense of losing something so central to your identity?

Do you immediately start searching for solutions, or do you allow yourself to sink into despair?

The Psychology of Loss

The psychological literature on grief reveals a truth particularly relevant to our experience: the process is neither linear nor universal, but rather intricate and deeply individual. Elisabeth Kübler-Ross's seminal 1969 work on the five stages of grief — denial, anger, bargaining, depression, and acceptance — while widely recognized, offers just one framework for understanding loss. More recent research highlights the flexibility and variation in how grief is experienced. A 2007 study published in *The Journal of the American Medical Association* found that most people experience fluctuating levels of distress over time, without following a fixed pattern of stages.

These academic frameworks help explain our collective experience. In many of the interviews I conducted, I observed the traditional five indicators as well as additional coping mechanisms.

Denial

The phenomenon of denial, explored earlier through embedded memory, found illustration in Nisha's (#29) case. She had completely buried her initial reaction to the collapse and only after our interview, 15 years after the collapse, did she finally confront that moment with her mother in the middle of the street when they both broke down in tears.

Anger and Disappointment

The collapse shattered the foundation of trust across all levels of the institution, from fresh analysts to seasoned veterans. Wynn (#28) witnessed the immediate aftermath: "I walked into the office and saw a colleague disconnecting his keyboard, trying to take his monitor apart next. I asked him what he was doing, and he said he was taking what was his."

Wynn was also stunned to see the coffee corners being stripped of everything—tea, coffee, sugar packets. "Something about people's survival instinct drove them to salvage whatever they could."

Feeling profoundly betrayed, Max (#16) found himself retreating to his parents' home in Germany — a return to square one that felt like a cruel twist of fate. "I had it all, working at one of the top five banks in the U.S., living in London, and suddenly I was back home arguing with my parents over dinner plans."

It was a humbling lesson in gratitude. Max continued searching for work in Germany, applying to countless positions and interviewing wherever he could. Eventually, he settled for a role at a traditional German bank. "The role itself wasn't the challenge — it was the cultural whiplash. I'd gone from the first-name basis of elite American institutions to the rigid formality of traditional German banking. Suddenly, I was at conservative German bank where I had to address managers formally."

Some still harbor anger 15 years later. Jay (#38) expressed it plainly, "I always felt that Lehman ruined my career. Starting at a top-tier bank only to end up at a second-rate institution left a lasting sense of disillusionment."

Bargaining

While traditional bargaining involves making deals with fate, our version took different forms. Kai (#12), who moved back to his home country, reflected: "I think going back home helped me find happiness again. Working fewer hours let me focus on myself in ways I hadn't before."

Milo (#22) found philosophical acceptance: "The more you dwell on it, the more you realize you're stuck. Life throws random events at you, and sometimes you get caught in them. There are worse things, like health crises. We all saw that during COVID."

Depression

Noa (#9) spoke about the overwhelming sadness and disappointment: "You spend your whole life working to get a great job at a top company, and then, just like that, it's gone"

Liam (#27) had two conversations shortly after the collapse that shook him. The first was with a recruiter offering a position at £25,000 a year—half the typical analyst salary at Lehman before bonuses. Stunned, Liam told the recruiter, "I'm willing to compromise, but that's half my current salary." The recruiter laughed and wished him luck.

The second conversation, which underscored how dire things were, was with a friend at another bank who told him, "If I submit your résumé, the only way you'll be hired is if I'm fired."

Isaac (#41) endured eight months of unemployment, describing it as the hardest time in his life. He refused job offers outside his field, even from hedge funds that later became giants. His wife supported him through the lengthy process.

Ray (#21) remembers the slow decline, "A few months later, it was clear things weren't improving. I was offered a severance package and left the bank by March 2009." When asked if he felt regret over missed opportunities, he admitted, "I'm not a man of many words, but it wasn't regret; it was shame."

Acceptance and Action

Those who ultimately distinguished themselves were the analysts who rapidly progressed from paralysis to pragmatism.

Isaac (#41) describes a surreal scene, all the analysts gathered in a room, collectively applying to new jobs, shouting out answers to each other. "What did you put for question 3 on Barclays' test?" One friend scored so poorly on a negative-marking test that the company called him in disbelief, inviting him to retest. Isaac advised him not to go.

Marco (#46) grappled with indecision on the day of the collapse. His father sternly advised him that thousands of people would now compete for a few positions and that acting first would secure an advantage.

Marco sent out over 100 résumés and secured a competitive edge before even going to the office later that day.

Lena (#13) moved with her family from east Europe to Canada at the age of 16 where she pursued her undergraduate studies. During her time at university, she spent a semester in Spain, where she secured a summer internship at Lehman in 2007, which led to her recruitment into the 2008 analyst class. Like all non-European analysts, Lena quickly realized she needed to find a solution. She interviewed anywhere she could and reached out to everyone she knew. "I had 20 days to find a job while thousands of us were competing for the same positions", she recalled. She secured several interviews with one of Canada's leading banks. In a very deliberate decision, she flew back to Canada for those interviews and ended up staying there. Incidentally, she is one of the few I spoke to who has remained at the same job all these years.

Milo (#22) swallowed his pride and started a new internship at a bank in India: "I was older than most interns and never thought I'd start over, but I understood the bank's position. The economy was harsh, and they got quality talent at a lower cost."

Determined to create value, Arjun (#14) continued his CPA studies begun at Nomura and kept himself busy working in cafés to avoid isolation. When the industry picked up again, he received two offers from Barclays—one in trading, one in research.

Remembering that his friend Milo was still jobless in India, Arjun, in a magnanimous gesture, brought Milo's résumé to his interview and secured him a position. Today, both remain in London's finance industry.

Before joining Lehman, Liam (#27) had turned down an internship at McKinsey in India. Realizing the need for strategic action, he asked a friend at McKinsey to deliver his résumé to the partner who had interviewed him. The friend obliged, and McKinsey handpicked four ex-Lehman analysts for hire.

Elara (#25), in particular, notes that she had to struggle to remain in finance. She was laid off twice during the economic crisis—first from Lehman and later from another bank, where she "survived" 15 rounds of layoffs until the unit she was in was ultimately dissolved, leading to her second dismissal. "If you are passionate about what you do, if you actually enjoy what you do, you will be good at your job," she stated, adding "And there are very few people, I think, that actually get up in the morning and love what they do"

While a collapse impacts everyone, it was particularly severe for Grace (#8).

Grace's (#8) story stands apart in its intensity. Raised in a family with a proud military tradition in China, her parents thrived in the late '90s during the economic boom. In 2000, she was sent to study in the UK, progressing to university, where she was recruited by the bank. "I didn't know what it was, but I assumed the pay was better than waitressing."

During her studies, she lost contact with her parents, hinting at a reality unknown in the Western world — people disappearing in China. It was only much later that she learned of their arrest and being sent to rehabilitation. Alone, she relied on her job for survival. Her parents only returned home after ten years.

The weekend before the collapse coincided with a major

Chinese holiday, where families gather. Her boyfriend's family invited her out, but she declined, glued to news updates, unable to process why this was happening to her. "The bank before us (Merrill Lynch) was rescued, the one after us (AIG) would be bailed out, and Lehman collapsed." The implications for her were dire. Without a job, her visa would soon expire, and returning to China might mean sharing her parents' fate. Driven by practicality, she announced to her fiancé that they needed to marry immediately to secure her residency.

In the months that followed, Grace reached out to anyone who could help her get an interview at Nomura. One day, she heard of an opening position. She guessed the manager's email address using his name and Lehman domain and sent a message. To her surprise, he replied: "Let's talk."

When asked why she wanted to work for his team she abandoned the typical aspirational answer for brutal honesty: "The job doesn't interest me, but I have no choice." The next day, she was accepted.

She never set foot in China again.

CHAPTER 14

Afterword

November 2024

Most books follow familiar arcs – the hero triumphs, finds love, or faces defeat. Business books typically build toward a single, profound revelation or watershed moment. But this isn't that kind of book.

What emerges instead is a tapestry of individual narratives, each threading its own path to resolution. And even these stories represent just a fraction of the whole – many voices are missing, whether because some declined to be interviewed or simply couldn't be tracked down in time.

Furthermore, with most protagonists still navigating their early forties, these narratives remain very much works in progress.

As I write this at 1:00 AM, trying to wrap up three years of work, I recognize this as less of a conclusion and more of an interim report on lives still unfolding.

That first interview in October 2021, marked the beginning of an unexpected journey. While the imperative to tell this story was clear, its ultimate destination remained tantalizingly uncertain.

I'm delighted to have completed this journey, and I hope it finds its audience. But even if it doesn't reach as many readers as I'd like, that's alright.

This book has served its purpose for me — helping me process and finally come to terms with the events of 2008 – arguably the most pivotal moment of my career. More importantly, it's helped me make peace with the choices I made during that time.

Looking back, the collapse of Lehman Brothers wasn't just about the end of a financial institution — it was about the beginning of a hundred different journeys. Some led back to banking, others to entirely new lives. But each path, whether chosen or forced upon us, taught its own lessons about resilience, reinvention, and what truly matters in life.

Perhaps what matters most isn't the story of an institution's collapse, but about our inherent ability to adapt when necessary. Some rewrote their stories by choice, others because circumstance left no alternative. Either way, new beginnings, whether chosen or forced, will surely lead to a hell of a ride.

Acknowledgments

This book would not exist without the support of countless individuals.

First and foremost, I'm deeply indebted to the members of Lehman Brothers' 2008 analyst class who shared their stories with me. Joining a virtual meeting out of nowhere to talk with someone you may or may not remember from years ago isn't an obvious choice.

I saw the hesitation in your expressions as I tried to explain what I was doing. I said it might be a book or a Netflix series. At least one of those promises came through. Thank you for trusting me with your experiences, both the painful and the triumphant.

To my early readers who weren't afraid to tell me when

my writing fell short - your push for clarity and honesty made this a better book. You know who you are, and your commitment to this project has been invaluable. Thank you for investing your time and wisdom so generously.

To Yael, who married a promising banker bound for London and found herself back in Israel with an unemployed husband within months: thank you for standing by me through it all. Together, we are invincible. And to my children, Guy, Nadav, and Michal: thank you for supporting this project over the years, for enduring countless hours of interviews, and for listening to endless stories of Lehman around the kitchen island, night after night. While you may not have gotten a London banker for a father, you helped a Tel Aviv dad follow his crazy, out-of-the-blue dream.

Dan

www.ingramcontent.com/pod-product-compliance
Lightning Source LLC
Chambersburg PA
CBHW071653240526
45469CB00021B/2286